Tutoring ESL* Students

*A Guide for Tutors (and Teachers)
in the Subject Areas*

*English as a Second Language

Marian Arkin
*LaGuardia Community College
The City University of New York*

Longman
New York & London

Tutoring ESL Students

Longman Inc., 19 West 44th Street, New York, N.Y. 10036
Associated companies, branches, and representatives throughout
the world.

Library of Congress Cataloging in Publication Data

Arkin, Marian, 1943-
  Tutoring ESL Students.

  (Longman series in college composition and communication)
    1. English language—Study and teaching (Higher)—Foreign
students.   2. Tutors and tutoring.   I.Title.   II. Title: Tutoring
E.S.L. students.
PE1128.A2A67   428'.007'1173   82-202
ISBN 0-582-28230-6   AACR2

Manufactured in the United States of America

CONTENTS

ACKNOWLEDGMENTS

Many people have contributed to the writing of this booklet, and I would like to thank them here. Charlotte Frede typed the manuscript; Linda Rios and Paul Arenson were the tutors who worked with me on the original pamphlet; Bert Eisenstadt at the Writing Center has consistently offered his support and advice; Linda Austin helped with research in the field of ESL; Doris Fassler, Linda Hirsch, Barbara Shollar, and Brian Gallagher reviewed the manuscript and offered invaluable suggestions for its improvement. None of this pamphlet, however, could have been written without the tenacity and patience of my ESL students at LaGuardia, who taught me how to teach them, and the continued enthusiasm and creativity of the Writing Center tutors, who over the years have been a constant source of energy and education for me.

PREFACE

Four years ago the number of non-native speakers of English at LaGuardia Community College, where I teach English and direct the Writing Center, began to increase markedly. We at the Writing Center found that the tutoring approaches we had developed over the years for native English speakers were not fully adequate for tutoring these ESL students. So we formed a committee of tutors knowledgeable about or interested in ESL, whose task was to come up with ways that the Writing Center could best meet the needs of ESL students. Also, two writing tutors studying for graduate degrees in English as a Second Language, joined with me to write a pamphlet for writing tutors on tutoring ESL students. My association with the field of English as a Second Language began then, and this booklet is an outgrowth of those meetings and later discussions with tutors and teachers about how best to help our ESL students.

Tutoring ESL Students is directed to tutors and teachers in all subject area labs who would like help in meeting the special learning needs of their ESL students. The booklet gives the reader background in each of the four areas in which ESL students encounter difficulty: listening, speaking, reading, and writing; it also offers methodologies and techniques tutors can use to deal with these problems. Each section contains a diagnostic test so that tutors can gauge how much help their students may actually need.

INTRODUCTION

To Whom Is This Book Addressed?

Suppose you are a history tutor. A student has come to you because he is doing poorly in American History. You find it difficult to understand his speech and wonder if the teacher is having a similar problem. When working with him, you notice that the student stumbles over words in the textbook, often stopping and asking what a word means. This marked hesitancy is surely interfering with his reading comprehension, you think. Or you may be a writing tutor. Your student speaks fairly well. She is animated and enthusiastic about her course. She likes the textbook and enjoys class discussions. "If only we didn't have to write so much," she moans. "Everything gets so mixed up when I write."

These tutees are both ESL (English as a Second Language) students, students who do not speak English as their native language.* These students may be

---

*When I refer to native speakers of English, I am talking about those people who speak English as a first language. Some non-native speakers may have been born in this country but have learned a language other then English as their first language. EFL (English as a Foreign Language) refers to those students

having academic difficulties similar to those of native speakers; however, they have additional problems
relating directly to their linguistic and cultural
displacement. You will find that, whatever your subject matter, in order to help them academically, you
must be aware of and address their "ESL" problems.

What Are the Special Problems of an ESL Student?

ESL students -- in fact, any students studying an academic subject in a language that is not native to them -- will find that their ability to be effective students directly corresponds to their linguistic ability in the target language (that is, the language in which the subject matter is being presented). Specifically, the ESL-related problems will interfere with their ability to listen, to speak, to read, and to write.

Obviously, students in some academic areas will be much more affected than others because they speak English as a second language: the sciences, especially mathematics and engineering, use a great many universal symbols which are the same whether the language is French, Japanese, Swahili, or English. Such symbols facilitate comprehension and problem-solving in these areas, particularly in verbal tasks. Conversely, courses that demand a great deal of expository writing or reading comprehension are very difficult for ESL students; therefore, it is not uncommon in schools with rigorous skills standards to find ESL students in their senior year who have still not passed all the reading and/or writing requirements of the college.

5

An additional problem for a number of ESL students is the psychological impact of living in a foreign country (and culture). Whether these students have permanently moved to this country or are here only temporarily, they must deal with the possible loneliness, insecurity, and alienation of being foreign. They will, in addition to learning a new language and new academic material, concurrently be learning new cultural material: dress, manners, customs.

It is a difficult, but by no means impossible, task to be an ESL student. Certainly the history of this country is, in many ways, a history of the migration and assimilation of peoples from different cultures. As a tutor, you are in a unique position to make such a task easier for this group of students. Classroom instructors typically have twenty to thirty students to teach. Their main responsibility is to instruct their students in the subject matter: physics, history, philosophy, engineering, and so forth. They probably will not be able to cater to the individual needs of their students, except where they coincide with those of the majority. So if three or four ESL students cannot understand the teacher because he speaks too fast, the teacher cannot slow down too much without the risk of boring the rest of the students. For the same reasons, the teacher cannot assign a simpler textbook to students who read English slowly (even when such texts may be available). You, however, can meet your students' individual needs. By understanding their unique problems you can help them gain confidence. By working with your ESL students on their linguistic skills in addition to their problems in the subject area that you tutor, you can help them compensate for their ESL-related difficulties.

But first you must recognize what the problems unique to ESL students are, and then you must learn strategies for dealing with them. This booklet should help you begin. It explores the four essential skills ESL students need -- listening, speaking, reading, and writing -- and how acquiring these skills can present special problems for the second language learner; it will aid you in recognizing these problems and understanding their nature; it presents ways you can help your students improve these skills. Finally, it discusses some pertinent issues in ESL teaching and tutoring. In all, its major goal is to give you extra tools so you can give your tutees the extra help only you, their tutor, can give them.

Setting Priorities

As in any tutoring situation, your first goal must be to set priorities, that is, to decide which of your tutee's needs should be addressed earlier than others. Perhaps you tutor social science and your tutee has brought in a history research assignment. The student, who has been in this country a year, understands the assignment, once you explain it, but needs your explanation because of reading problems. This student obviously needs practice in reading and you find, once a rough draft of the paper is written, she needs work in writing as well. But what of the subject matter? If you spend too much time on reading and writing, will you have enough time to tutor social science? You may be a math tutor. A student brings in a math problem he cannot solve. This ESL student has trouble with pronunciation. You have to strain to understand what he says. Should you spend time helping the student speak more clearly? After all, the student came to you to work on math, not speaking.

Both students need tutoring in their subject areas _and_ in ESL-related areas. The first student is effectively blocked from doing required classwork and, therefore, you ought to be spending some part of each session on reading and writing. The second student is not impeded by speaking difficulties, although these obviously hold him back from active participation in the class. You might want to work on pronunciation, but only if time permits. In both cases, you and your tutee must set priorities, must decide what is crucial and what can wait. Since your first responsibility is to tutor your subject area, you must make your student's comprehension of the subject area your first goal. You cannot do everything. If your student has extensive reading, writing, speaking, or listening problems, you should try to find him or her appropriate help with an ESL tutor, a reading tutor, a writing tutor, or a speech tutor.*

Do not be overwhelmed by all the material offered you in this book. It is meant to give you background, so you understand why your ESL students have the problems they do and so you can anticipate related difficulties that might arise during tutoring; and it is meant to provide you with a wide variety of techniques, so you can have as large a choice as possible when you do decide you need to address ESL-related problems.

---

*If a tutor is not available in these areas, you might want to refer to Tutoring Reading and Academic Survival Skills and The Writing Tutor, published by Longman in this series.

LISTENING

Those of you whose field is not Linguistics or Second Language Acquisition may think it odd to consider the linguistic skills of listening, speaking, reading, and writing as individual entities. How can one separate four such interrelated skills? Yet, while they are interrelated, they are also unique skills, acquired separately in different ways by individual learners. Learning to perceive them separately, then, is one way you can learn to recognize problems your tutees may be having in these areas.

To understand listening, we might best contrast it with hearing. Hearing involves the perception of sounds. Some of these sounds may be in meaningful patterns, that is, words, phrases, and sentences. Some may be abstract, unconnected, apparently meaningless. However, when we listen, we actively process what we hear: we differentiate some sounds from others; we interpret the meaning of words, phrases, and sentences. Listening, then, demands special abilities beyond the physiological ability to hear; it involves an ability to concentrate on sounds, to recognize them in and out of their context and to understand what is being communicated so that one can respond appropriately.

Listening can be difficult for the ESL student because it is particularly difficult to control the listening experience. (One may ask the speaker to slow down, but such a request, especially in front of a class, is often embarrassing. And, of course, one cannot slow down the presentation of the material when it is on film or tape.) Listening is especially problematic because it creates a vicious cycle: when an unfamiliar word is introduced, it may cause students to panic about missing material in the lecture or discussion and such panic eventually does cause them to miss material. It is all the more difficult for ESL students to remember what they are listening to, even while they are listening, because they are trying so hard to work out the meaning of new ideas. Their frequent confusion and anxiety while listening makes it hard for them to challenge or support what they are hearing or to relate it to what they already know. Moreover, listening skills are grounded on prior knowledge -- knowledge of the language, of the speaker, of his or her world and circumstances, and of the cultural context, including the meaning of non-verbal cues. A native speaker can understand a lot without actively listening simply through this prior knowledge. For example, native speakers of English probably would not have to listen to every word of a discussion about the historic significance of Abraham Lincoln to get the speaker's gist because they have either read about or studied Lincoln at some point prior to the conversation. However, persons unfamiliar with extra-linguistic cues will have less information to go on and will thus have to depend more on their knowledge of the language which, imperfect as it is for them, is all they have.

Listening Strategies

What can you, as tutor, do to help the student "listen" better?

Be Aware That Listening Can Be a Major Problem. This may not be as easy as it sounds. Many ESL students are ashamed of poor listening skills and may not tell you they do not understand you or the teacher. It is fairly easy to fake understanding if the only feedback asked for is a nod, smile, or yes/no answer. Some ESL students do not know when they have misunderstood. They may believe they caught the gist of what was said, or they may believe a word means one thing when it really means something else.

One clue that your students may have a listening problem is difficulty following directions. If your

tutees come with a paper or exam in which they have
not done what was asked of them, find out if the instructions were verbal or written and review them with
the student, if possible. Look for other clues, like
inappropriate responses to what you say or problems
in turning to the right section of a book. Ask students to show they understand what you've said by
having them take an active part in the tutorial (e.g.,
answering questions about the material, generating
discussion). You might, also, want to make up a
listening diagnostic, like the one below:

Directions: Ask your tutees to answer the following
               questions as you read them aloud. (Do
               not permit them to look at the ques-
               tions.)

1. What is your name and major field?

2. What courses have you taken in your major
   field?

3. What classes are you taking this term?

4. How do you like them?

5. Why have you come for tutoring?

7. Write down the names of your three favorite
   books.

8. How did you hear about the tutoring center?

9. How do you get from your home or dorm to the
   center?

10. What did you eat for dinner last night?

Notice that none of the questions asked for a yes, no, or single-word answer, so as to give the student less opportunity to "guess" an answer. Also, none required any special knowledge, so what emerges pertains purely to listening competence. If your student has gotten six or more of these questions wrong, he or she needs specialized tutoring; if there is an ESL lab at your college, you should send the student there and/or urge the student to enroll in an ESL course. If he or she got barely any wrong, the listening problem is minimal. Between three and five wrong denotes listening problems that are surely interfering with classwork, so pay special attention to possible listening problems when you tutor this student.

Speak Clearly and Pause Frequently, but Do Not Speak Too Slowly. ESL students need more time to process information than native speakers, as they are attempting to decode a spoken message; therefore, you should resist the temptation to speak with exaggerated slowness and distinctness which can distort the blendings and segmentation of normal speech. In addition, a message spoken at an exaggeratedly slow rate can actually interfere with a person's ability to recall -- by the time the message is completed, the listener may have lost track of what was said at the beginning. Instead, you should take advantage of the pauses that occur in conversational speech to give tutees a chance to process what they are hearing. You can lengthen the pauses and/or insert more pauses -- but always in a place that makes sense. In this way, students are given a chance both to interpret the message at a less hurried rate, and, at the same time, to practice listening to the actual sound of speech as it is spoken in the "real world."

If students have trouble recognizing a specific word or group of words, you may want to stop and break it down for them by explaining new words, repeating what you've said in other words, or giving the phrase to them word by word, so they can recognize its individual components. Many times, listening comprehension problems occur not because students don't know the individual words, but because they don't re-cognize them within the stream of sound that is speech. Often, just writing down a word for them allows students to recognize the word. It's important, though, after you have broken the message down into smaller units, to put the word or phrase back into its phonological "context," so students can hear it again as they would outside the lesson.

Give Students Conversation Practice, Time When You Just Chat. Tutoring is a unique time when students can practice listening to casual conversation, the kind that will be most common in their lives. In tutoring they can control their listening activity by asking you to stop, slow down, and repeat or explain a word or phrase. Thus, it is a time when they can listen without anxiety. The tutorial session is also a good time to encourage students to open up about problems they may be having in adjusting to their new environment. If you have trouble thinking of things to talk about, try focusing on cultural differences; such topics usually elicit interesting conversation. The following aspects of culture make for lively discussion: dress, clothes, dating and marriage, male and female prerogatives, children and schooling, food and eating customs, leisure time activities, cultural values, the arts.

Give Students Practice Mini-lectures (10-minutes maximum) on Relevant Classwork to Help Them Understand Class Lectures Better. Be sure to ask them questions at intervals to be certain they are understanding you.

Use These Lectures to Give Tutees Practice in Note-taking. Check their notes and, if inadequate, point out where there are problems, without correcting. Then give them the lecture again.

Note-taking is a particular problem for ESL students because the "listening" it entails demands the ability to understand what is being said (or read), to grasp its main ideas, and to paraphrase this information. Be aware that ESL students often attempt to write down an instructor's lecture verbatim, resulting in the student's missing much of the information. You can monitor the student's note-taking processes by reading aloud passages from the text, having the student take notes, and then reviewing these notes.

Since effective listening is, in part, based on extra-linguistic knowledge, Prepare Your Tutees by Scanning Textbook Assignments and Going Over Any Cultural Information the Students Might Not Know Because Foreign Born. For example, a 20th-century American literature class might talk about the importance of certain cities or areas as locales of literary movements: e.g., Chicago, Hollywood, Brooklyn, Harlem. If you talk to your tutees about the cities, historically and culturally, they will have a much better chance of understanding class discussion than if they were left to wonder about the image and connotations of meat markets in Chicago, film studios in Hollywood, and the Brooklyn Bridge and Harlem in New York City.

Help Your Students Build an English-language Vocabulary. ESL students will often not recognize English vocabulary native speakers take for granted. Encourage your students to keep a list or index file cards containing words they didn't know, with definitions and a sentence in which the word is used. You might also quiz tutees from time to time on newly acquired vocabulary and encourage them to circle and write down new words they see in newspapers, advertisements, etc.

Help Your Tutees Anticipate Any Special Jargon or Other Linguistic References That Might Occur in Class Discussion. For instance, a social science class discussing education theories might refer to American public school education; a lesson on American music might refer to Dixieland or Motown. (In the former case, the person might have no real understanding of a compulsory educational system supported by the state; those educated under the British system might even assume that this meant a private school system.) Look in the syllabus or textbook for words that might need review.

Use Some of the Following Techniques to Build Up Your Tutee's Listening Skills:

Records

There are special ESL records available which feature controlled listening exercises that gradually increase in difficulty. If your students have severe listening problems see if you can direct them to an ESL tutor who will probably have access to this material. "Spoken word" records can be useful in giving your tutees additional listening practice. See if your library has any records pertinent to your subject area (e.g., for literature students, Dylan Thomas reading A Child's Christmas in Wales).

Recorded Conversation

Tapes of yourself or others in actual conversation can give your students much needed conversation practice. If you make a transcript of your tape you can assign the listening as homework and go over the transcript during the session, discussing any difficult terms, phrasings, or pronunciation. Also, tape record a relevant section of the subject area and ask students to write or speak a summary showing what they understood. Recordings of news broadcasts or talk shows are also extremely useful.

Dictation

Dictation is sometimes referred to as a bridge between speaking and writing because it involves directly transcribing the sounds one hears. Here are some ways dictation can give your students listening practice:

On a beginning level, you might dictate sentences pertaining to your subject matter, and ask your students to read each transcribed sentence back to you; that way you can give them immediate feedback on each sentence; most of your students will probably be intermediate or advanced listeners, and it would be more helpful to them if you dictated longer paragraphs from the textbook. If you notice that your tutee has trouble hearing a particular sound, for example, "ed" endings in the past tense, you should then load sentences and paragraphs with these sounds, as in the following paragraph:

> When the young girl toppled down the stairs
> everyone laughed. She looked so funny as
> she bounced and bounced and bounced down
> the stairs. Luckily, she landed safely,
> but she cried anyway. However, the stairs
> were padded with a heavy rug which cushioned
> her fall.

Read your dictation two times at normal speed, pausing at punctuation marks and in between sense groups (clauses, phrases, sentences) to give students a chance to write. Say punctuation as it occurs (e.g., I know comma nonetheless comma you are happy period). You may ask them to repeat silently to themselves what they heard before writing it down. Ask them to read it through at the end, checking for lexical and grammatical sense. Then give them a transcript so they can check what they have written.

A way of varying the degree of difficulty is to vary the length of the clause or phrase -- that is, to decrease or increase the amount of text read in between pauses.

Yet another approach to dictation is to read a passage (from your textbook or written by you from text material) and to ask students to write down the sense of it in their own words. Have them read the paraphrase; discuss discrepancies.

"Drawing-a-Dictation" asks you to dictate a picture, a map, a diagram -- anything that requires tutees to understand details and follow directions -- so that they can practice listening to and drawing these details. Then you can check their drawings against your description. Again, try to think of visualizations from the work you are tutoring, e.g., a physics diagram, or a description of a painting. If nothing else comes to mind, describe an area near campus. Try to have a drawing of your dictation ready so your tutee can compare theirs with yours.

SPEAKING

In linguistic terminology, listening asks the tutee to "decode" or interpret what others are trying to communicate, while speaking asks them to "encode," that is to put what they have to say into the linguistic code of the community which they are addressing. Although some learners find it easier to speak than to listen, because in speaking they control the content of the message and the speed at which it is delivered, speaking can be the most potentially humiliating experience for a foreign-born student because of all the opportunities inherent in this activity to misuse words, to mispronounce words, and to make mistakes in verbal codes. For speech is essentially a social act. We speak to a listener or listeners, and the speaking act communicates much more than a literal message. Speech codes reveal education, worldliness, social class, even state of mind. Your tutees need to learn to control those codes, to learn when to use colloquialisms (like "bucks" for "dollars," "heavy" for "deep"), polite and impolite verbal address (e.g., when an instructor should be addressed as "teacher," "m'am," "sir," "professor," "Dr.," "Ms.," "Mr."), and what common non-verbal cues mean (when staring is permissible, when one should shake hands).

Your tutees also need to pronounce English so that faulty pronunciation doesn't interfere with their ability to be understood. Pronunciation may be especially difficult for them, especially if they have come to this country after their childhood years. When we speak, we mimic what we hear, but we tend to hear sounds according to the sound pattern of our native language. Thus new speakers of a language may mishear sounds if these don't exist in their native tongue.

As a tutor, you can give your tutees a comfortable forum in which they can practice speaking at ease. As with the listening activity, the tutorial may be the only place where your tutees can practice speaking English and do so unselfconsciously. You should make them aware that, as speaking will play such a large part in their academic lives, it is appropriate that it be part of the tutorial.

Speaking Strategies

Speech errors, unlike those in listening, are immediately obvious. What Can Be Helpful, However, Is to Classify the Kinds of Problems Your Tutees Are Having so You Can Devise Ways of Working on Them.

The following diagnostic should help you do that:

Directions: Ask your tutee a series of fairly
              simple questions like the ones
              below. He or she should answer
              orally in complete sentences.

1.   Talk about the jobs you have had.

2.   What do you think of this school, city,
     country, etc.?

3.   Tell me about your country (a holiday in
     your country, food, schools, etc.).

4.   What did you do this past weekend?

Listen to his or her answers for the following:

1.   ability to answer in clear, meaningful units

2.   ability to answer grammatically, and in
     complete sentences

3.   ability to pronounce vowel sounds and initial
     consonant sounds intelligibly

Problems in (1) point to semantic difficulties.
Your tutees may not have acquired a large enough English vocabulary (or may have mislearned some words).
Or they may know single words but may not be comfortable putting words together in phrases and sentences.
Finally, your tutees may have a book knowledge of
English but may need to learn to speak idiomatic English.   If your tutees insert a number of words from
their native languages, they are obviously having
vocabulary difficulties.

Problems in (2) point to syntactic problems.

Grammar, in general, shall be discussed later in this booklet; however, if your tutees are having problems at this very simple grammatical level of answering questions in complete sentences, recommend they get additional help (e.g., an ESL class or tutor). Do let your tutees know, however, that when we speak we do not often speak in complete sentences and our ability to be understood is in no way impaired. The stipulation that tutees speak in complete sentences is for diagnostic purposes only.

Problems in (3) point to pronunciation difficulties. A good many severe pronunciation problems should be handled by a specialist; it is really not your province to work with your tutees on incomprehensible, or nearly incomprehensible speech. However, you can help them improve pronunciation so that it doesn't draw attention to itself in academic situations.

Usually It Is Better Not to Correct Students as They Speak. The last thing you want to do is make them feel self-conscious about every word they utter. Instead, pick out an incorrect pattern of pronunciation (e.g., using the "ee" sound for the "I" sound, as "theenk" for "thInk") and work with them on this pattern after the regular tutorial lesson is completed. When students use incorrect words or idioms, write down incorrect usage and discuss it after the lesson.

Some students, however, might want the tutor to correct them as they speak, or designate part of the lesson (5 or 10 minutes) time when the tutor can stop and correct them. There are many ways to do this. The tutor can simply repeat the phrase or sentence in question, correcting the mistakes. Or the tutor can give clues to where a mistake has been made, and what kind of mistake it is.

The Tutorial Is a Good Place to Discuss Social Rules Concerning What We Can and Cannot Say. Questions of verbal decorum may arise from a teacher's comment on a paper ("Don't use the colloquialism 'man,' as in 'well, man,' in a class essay.") or because the class may have responded oddly to something the student said. For example, students may have picked up profanities or "vulgar" idioms on the street, and may be actually using them correctly in a functional but inappropriate way -- often without knowing exactly what they are saying. The tutor is a good person to explain what the words mean as well as the contexts in which these words might be used. For instance, there is a great difference between saying "mess up," "screw up," and "fuck up," -- none of which would be used in a paper, but all of which

26

might be used at one time or another by a native speaker of "good breeding." It's important to note that native speakers can "get away with" a lot more than a foreigner, not merely in terms of vulgar idioms, but also in terms of basic grammatical correctness.

Teach Your Students the Phonetic System in Their Dictionaries. With a knowledge of phonetics they can look up words that they are unsure of and can sound them out themselves.

Phonetics can be especially useful if students don't hear the difference between sounds. In Spanish, for instance, the sound of "y" in you and "j" in June are merely different ways of saying the same sound, which in Spanish is represented by the letter j and pronounced like our letter h. As a result students literally may not hear the difference between the two sounds in English. They may not see what the fuss is about when they say "jou" for "you" or "Yune" for "June." You can write down the two letters (or the phonetic representations of the letters) and label them "1" and "2." You might then say a word (real or nonsensical) and ask the student to tell which sound has been used. Once the student can hear the difference, roles can be reversed and the student can practice saying words with the designated

27

sound while you give feedback on whether the sound was "1" or "2."

Since people new to phonetic symbols and how they indicate pronunciation can find the process difficult, be sure to practice the method with your tutee.

Practice Sounding Out Difficult Consonant or Vowel Sounds by Using "Contrastive Pronunciation"; that is, contrast the sound as pronounced in the student's native language with the sound in English (e.g., the French or Spanish "qui," which corresponds to the English sound "key," can be used to clarify the "K" sound).

It Can Also Be Helpful to Examine for Yourself How You Physically Make (or Articulate) a Given Sound and Then Try to Help Students Reproduce the Sound by showing them how to manipulate vocal machinery: shape of mouth, position of tongue, use or nonuse of "voice,"* etc. For example, many students have difficulty with the th sounds in think and this, often because they are unused to, and perhaps uncomfortable

---

*Voice is a technical term that refers to the part that vocal chords play in the production of a sound: most vowels and some consonants (b, g, d, for example) are produced by vibrating of the vocal chords; others (p, t, f) require that the vocal chords not vibrate. Problems with voice in English are anaogous to difficulties English speakers have with the gutteral pronunciations of German and the nasal pronunciations of French.

with, the idea of sticking their tongues in between their teeth. The tutor can assure them that not only is it perfectly polite to do so, but that they must do so in order to make the sound correctly.

Give Your Students Questioning Practice. One of the things that suffers when students have poor speaking skills is their ability to ask for what they need and about what they cannot understand. For instance, students may be having trouble understanding a particular concept but will be too embarrassed (or perhaps cannot find the words) to ask the teacher to go over it. Or students may have a question or may disagree about a point in the teacher's lecture but may not be able to challenge the point. Read them a controversial passage on the subject matter (or lecture to them on something interesting and relevant) and ask them to prepare five to ten questions. Encourage them to question you whenever necessary and to write down questions they were unable to ask in class for discussion in the tutorial.

Try the Following Techniques for Giving Your Students Further Speaking Practice:

Aural Taping

Aural (sound) tapes are useful to capture conversation in the tutorial for playback and analysis. Your students can also use the tape at home to practice their own pronunciation against a master tape made commercially, or by you.

Video Taping

While the aural tape can capture only what you and/or your tutees say, the video can capture non-verbal behavior as well. It can be especially reassuring to students to see how much better they communicate in English than they think they do.

Roleplaying

Simulating a problem situation in class can give your students solutions to deal with it, along with additional conversation practice. (See Chapter 7 in The Tutor Book for instructions on roleplaying.) For example, if your students freeze up every time the teacher calls on them, recreate the situation. Give students a chance to play both teacher and student. That way when the real situation comes about, it will be less awesome.

Interviewing

If you are tutoring more than one person, ask your tutees to interview each other (i.e., ask questions) on something pertaining to classwork. For example, one can question another on a chapter assigned for homework, on the items on a test, or in the classwork.

Peer-critiquing

Peer-critiquing, like interviewing, is

valuable not only because it reinforces content, but also because it involves a great deal of relevant conversation practice. In peer-critiquing students evaluate each other's work, usually written work. You, as tutor, can guide this process by giving your tutees specific things to look for, e.g., in an essay: main idea, development, grammar. Students tend to learn a lot about the subject they are critiquing; they also gain a feeling of authority and ease (a critical voice) about the subject matter that can only help their speaking ability.

This technique can also be used for oral work; if you are working with a group, each student can listen for how group members use a particular grammar or pronunciation point (-ed endings, third-person singular -s). Students can evaluate how others did at the end of the session.

Reports

As homework, ask your students to prepare a report on something pertinent to the subject matter of the tutorial. If your tutees have to give an oral report in class, have them practice it with you several times, recording it aurally or on video-tape if possible. Urge your tutees to write out the report, using capital letters and triple space, and to underline any words that should be emphasized. If the students' pronunciation is especially poor, have them write problem words phonetically.

Oral Reading

From time to time ask your students to read out key paragraphs from the textbook, then summarize them in their own words. They should read the paragraph to themselves before summarizing because it is difficult to ingest meaning when reading aloud -- a foreign speaker especially tends to concentrate on pronunciation rather than meaning.

All of the above strategies stress the meaningful integration of subject matter with conversation practice. Speaking, as mentioned earlier, is done with people; it usually demands an audience, and you are the best audience the student can have because you are not judgmental, you are interested in what the student says, and you are in a position to be a model of good speaking habits. Students may not have such an opportunity outside of the tutorial. The classroom tends to be anxiety ridden for the non-fluent, and the home, although potentially a good place to practice English conversation, is also a place of comfort where students may need to speak their native language to relax from the pressures of trying to function in English all day. So never feel you are taking time from the real subject of the tutorial by practicing conversation. Oral fluency is a crucial key to academic survival.

READING

Of the four areas of verbal ability under consideration here, reading is perhaps the least difficult for an ESL student: like listening, reading involves decoding a linguistic message, that is, interpreting what is being communicated by the writer; however, when we read we normally have a certain amount of time to think about what is written. We can use this time to look words up in a dictionary, or to ask someone what something means; and we can reread several times until the meaning is clear. Therefore, reading is not normally so anxiety provoking for ESL students as speaking or listening because the activity is usually more in their control than are the others.

Still, reading is not easy for ESL students. First, a great many of their exams are timed, and these tests ask them to interpret written material precisely, both to read directions and to analyze written material. They must find a way to read quickly enough so that their performance on the exam is not handicapped. Second, reading does not usually give students immediate feedback. They may read and think they understand, but unless questioned (and corrected) on the material afterwards, they may not find, until a bad grade on a paper or test, that they have misunderstood a section of a work, or even the entire work. Finally, people tend to read contrastively, that is, they apply what they know about their native language to the new language. Equivalent or different vocabulary and syntax can help or hinder the immediate apprehension and decoding of something the student is reading, since we tend to make predictions about what is coming next based, at least partially, on semantic and syntactic patterns. For example, a German student, seeing the word "cold," will probably think of its German cognate kalt and thus he will be able to understand its meaning in a sentence without having actually learned it. But, words, although cognates, often change over time, and one cannot count on cognates in different languages to retain the same meaning. (One expects bekommen in German to mean "become" in English. However, instead it means "to receive.")

An ESL student from a country which does not use the Roman alphabet (e.g., China, Israel, Russia), on the other hand, will have a different problem in deciphering new symbols. Since English is a Germanic language at base, with strong influences from Latin and French, students who speak a language outside the Germanic and Roman Language groups will naturally

34

lack those grammatical and syntactic clues available to people whose native language somewhat resembles English.

Reading is, however, crucial to survival in college, so your role as tutor is not only to help tutees understand what they read in their courses, but to make reading generally easier and more pleasureable for them. (For additional ways to deal with reading problems, refer to <u>Tutoring Reading and Academic Survival Skills</u> published in the same series.)

Reading Strategies

<u>You Can Use What Is Called a Cloze Passage to Test Whether Tutees' Reading Material Is Too Difficult for Them</u>. Simply take a passage from one of their textbooks, or from a textbook in the same subject area, and, except for the first sentence, delete every sixth word, leaving a standard-sized blank. What you give students will be similar to this one:

Photography is sometimes called the art of making the real look more real. One certainly agrees when looking_____the works of Ansel Adams. _____great American photographer has captured_____spectacular natural beauty of the

_____. His shots of the Rockies, _____ example, have startling beauty which _____ made many native Americans see _____ mountains for the first time. _____ photographs of trees, lakes, snow-covered _____ turn these natural objects into _____ of supernatural wonder. Adams accomplishes _____ in three ways. First, he _____ the light, primarily by using _____ yellow filter, so that it _____ unbottled onto the object being _____. Second, he composes the elements _____ the picture to emphasize their _____. Thirdly, he is a visionary; _____ is able to pick out _____ appears commonplace to most of _____ and to realize and then _____ capture its special qualities. That _____ ethereal quality, vision, cannot, like _____ and composition, be learned. It _____ the talent that separates the _____ from the artist.

In scoring a cloze, count right any word that makes sense within the context of the passage, and that is in the correct grammatical form (tense, number, etc).

Before giving a cloze to students, introduce them to the concept by giving them a few simple sentences, like the ones below, for words that are relatively easy to guess, or which can be at least narrowed down to a few likely answers:

1. I'm really tired today because I stayed up too _____ last night.
2. Her dress was made of _____.
3. She _____ the piano very well.

You can also use cloze passages as exercises, for practice. Students can do a cloze after reading (or hearing) a complete passage. Or they can read the cloze without filling in the blanks and answer questions given by the tutor. In this way students see that they can still understand much of a passage without knowing every word. (This will help students to break the habit of word-for-word reading, and so allow them to increase their speed.)

Another Way to Encourage Reading Fluency Is to Urge Your ESL Students to Read Things Through Once, Stopping Only to Underline Words They Don't Know, and Not to Look Any Words Up. If they stop they may find out what a particular word means while forgetting the gist of the entire paragraph or essay. Once they have a sense of what a particular passage means, they can go back and look up the underlined words, then reread with enhanced comprehension.

37

Show Your Tutees How to Guess Meaning Through
Context and Grammatical Structure. Reassure them
that it is not essential to know the meaning of every
word, that one can work out relative meaning by
looking at surrounding words and grammatical clues
to structure. For example, in the following passage
by Joseph Conrad, nonsense words have replaced some
real words to simulate how words appear when they
are not known to your tutees:

> In exterior he otiled a butcher in a poor
> neighborhood, and his kars had a look of
> sleepy cunning. He carried his fat loomph
> with ostentation on his short legs and
> during the time his gang infested the sta-
> tion spoke to no one but his siltoh.
>
> > Heart of Darkness
> > New York: Bantam, 1960, p. 35.

They can tell the first word, "otiled," is a
verb by its position next to the pronoun and by its
regular -ed ending. Since the passage is talking
about his looks, it makes sense he is being compared
to a butcher in looks: hence the word is "looks
like" or, as is the case, "resembled." The second
word, "kars," is easier to interpret since the word
cunning is so often used with "look" and eyes are
often described as "sleepy." "Loomph" can be more

38

difficult to work out. What is fat and carried on legs? They might guess "stomach" or "trunk" and be fairly close to the read word, "paunch." Finally, who is the "siltoh," the only one to whom this fat, ugly man confided? Students will know it is a noun since it comes after a possessive pronoun, but the context doesn't really give them enough clues. Indeed, it is virtually impossible to guess the word. However, having worked most of the passage out by themselves, they would need only to quickly look at the dictionary (or in this case, the original passage) to find the definition of the word "nephew."

Go Over Word Formation with Students, Especially Root Formation: a knowledge of common suffixes and prefixes can help them to figure out meaning themselves. You might make this information part of a general lesson on how to use the dictionary, the history of word borrowings, etc.

Teach Students to Recognize the Components of Paragraphs and Essays. They should learn how to find the main ideas, subordinating ideas, and details supporting those ideas. They should know what a thesis is and how it functions in an essay. They should learn to recognize introductions and conclusions, rhetorical strategies, like narration, comparison/contrast, process, and methods of development. They should be able to pinpoint structural and lexical clues to these components, e.g., lexical clues like _in general_, _for example_, _on the other hand_. By understanding how an essay is put together, they will be better able to anticipate what is included in a reading, even if they don't understand all the vocabulary.

Give Your Tutees Exposure to Different Kinds of Test Questions and the Language That Is Used in Them. Make them familiar with key words like _define_, _analyze_, _list_, _compare/contrast_, _show_, _prove_, _examine_, _explore_. Familiarize them with different kinds of test structures, e.g., essay, multiple choice, short answer, fill-in, perhaps by giving them examples of tests using these structures.

Give Your Tutees Experience with Timed Reading, for example in a trial test situation where they have to read and interpret a passage and answer a question in a certain amount of time.

If At All Possible, Give Your Tutees Guided Reading Questions Before They Read Difficult Material for Class. (This will be easier to do if you have taken the course yourself and are familiar with the textbook.) These questions should focus on the main points in the passage and should guide students to look at key concepts. Or look over the title, chapter headings, pictures or diagrams in the text, and an introductory paragraph with tutees; then have them generate questions of their own to be answered in the course of reading.

In the Same Way, Question Your Tutees About What They Have Read, Asking Them Questions That Will Point Up Their Understanding of Significant Details and Major Themes.

If Your Tutees Are in a Special Field, e.g., Data Processing, Psychology, Have a Dictionary of That Field's Jargon; Some of These are Specifically Geared to Foreign Speakers. Most assuredly, they will need to know specialized terms and it can be helpful to go over the most common ones. (Look over the textbook or syllabus to ascertain which words are crucial to the term's work.)

WRITING

Writing represents the greatest problem for ESL college students because it is in writing out a thought or concept, answering a question in writing, structuring an essay that problems in all four areas come together. Writing is the permanent record of what we have heard, what we say and think, and what we read, and it is one of the major ways a student is judged in college. It is the outward manifestation of all knowledge and students are expected to do it carefully, precisely, even elegantly.

An ESL student will most certainly have problems with vocabulary. Idioms, of course, which are so difficult to translate because they are not literal, are a major source of error. Your tutees will probably have trouble finding the right word. They may use a dual language (e.g., English-Spanish) dictionary or a thesaurus and the word they choose, often a direct translation from their native language, may be slightly inappropriate. For example, a student may say "I desire to pass this course," having found the dictionary defines "desire" as "to want" and not realizing the sensual connotation of the word. Probably the hardest group of vocabulary words for ESL students is prepositions (e.g., at, in, to, of, for) because the difference between them is so subtle and, therefore, difficult to explain, and because dictionary definitions are so multiple and confusing.

Although your ESL students may have traditional grammar problems, depending on their knowledge of their native language's grammar and the relation between English grammar and the grammar of their native language, their major problems will center around verbs. English has a great number of irregular verbs and there is no way to learn which verbs are irregular and what their forms are except by memorizing them. ESL students also tend to have problems with the third-person present-tense singular, since it is the only consistently inflected form in English. They might also have problems with plurality, sometimes pluralizing an adjective or adding an s to an already plural form (e.g., childrens). Spanish speakers often have trouble with the subject pronoun, omitting it in English because, as it is implied by the verb, it is commonly omitted in Spanish (e.g., Is a very good party). They also have trouble with the relative pronoun because, while in English there are several forms, depending on what is being described (who, which, that), in Spanish there is only one (que). Chinese speakers, on the other hand, have trouble with all English inflections because their language has so few. Therefore, tense or plurals may present

43

problems for Chinese students since verbs and nouns do not change in Chinese to show tense and plural shifts.

Finally, ESL students tend to have problems with fluency. Not being familiar with the sound of the language, and the way words group together in phrases and clauses, their writing will sometimes be awkward, clumsy or confusing.

The following section will address itself to the above problems. For ways to deal with other writing problems your ESL student may have, refer to The Writing Tutor, published in this same series.

Writing Strategies

Use Writing Students Have Done in Class, e.g., a Composition, an Essay Exam, to Diagnose Your Tutee's Writing Problems. Teachers will probably have written comments about the writing to let you and students know what instructors think needs improvement. Also, written in class or for a class, a sample will accurately reflect what matters need most urgently to be addressed in the tutorial.

However if no such writing sample is available, ask your tutees to write for you. Try to choose a topic related to the subject area; then ask students to write 200-300 words on the topic. A 200-300 word essay should give you sufficient material to diagnose what kinds of ESL-related writing problems need work. Look especially for areas treated in this section -- word usage, grammar, and fluency -- because these are the major trouble areas for ESL students.

Word Usage   If your tutees consistently use words incorrectly, try to analyze what kinds of words are misused, and how they came to use the words they chose. Incorrect word usage usually fits into one of four categories: idioms, prepositions, articles, and general vocabulary. Since students make errors in these categories for different reasons, each will be discussed separately here.

    Idioms   An idiom is a compound word (e.g., greenhouse) or group of words that is understood to mean something more than or different from the sum of its parts. It has grown to mean something over the years other than its literal, dictionary translation. "Side by side" is an idiom, as is a figure of speech such as "turn over a new leaf." Native speakers of a language don't normally think of an expression as idiomatic unless asked about it. They are so used to hearing it, it sounds perfectly natural to them. In fact, they are often made aware that an expression is an idiom when a non-native speaker laughs or is puzzled by something they say. Idioms are, however, extremely difficult for non-native speakers because they cannot be anticipated and often cannot be translated, at least not merely by checking each component of the idiom in a dictionary. They must be painstakingly noted, translated, memorized, and used.

You can help your tutees in the following ways:

1. You can point out idioms used by you, in the textbook, or commonly in your field.

2. You can explore their meaning with your tutee. Often that will mean looking up the word history in the Oxford English Dictionary or figuring out what the idiom means literally (e.g., "pie in the sky" means highly unlikely, as unlikely as it would be to find pie in the sky).

3. Help your students to memorize idioms by using them yourself and inviting students to use them. (e.g., "Would you say total employment is pie in the sky?")

4. Ask your tutees to write sentences using selected idioms, for it is often in written usage that the idiom appears clumsy, awkward, and out of place.

Prepositions Prepositions usually modify nouns or verbs to express some kind of relationship, either temporal or spatial. Their meaning is often difficult to explain and, therefore, difficult for the ESL students to ascertain. One of the best ways to help your students understand prepositions is to help them see the relationships these words imply. The following strategies and techniques should help you do this:

1. Roleplay Write a brief scenario laden with prepositions (preferably related to your field). For example, you can ask your tutee to talk (and act out) a lab experiment such as the following:

> I wash the test tube in soap and water
> for five minutes. Then I take it to
> the table and fill it with carbolic
> acid. After thoroughly shaking the
> test tube, I can add the chemicals.

Or ask tutees to write their own situations to act out, making certain these skits have a number of prepositions.

2. Ask your tutees to pick a location you both know and draw a simple map of that area. Then they should dictate how to get from one location to another while you draw the route on the map. (e.g., "First go down A Street, around the corner

take a left, and before the light make a right.")

3. <u>Ask your tutees to hide ten items</u> near the room
and then to help you find all ten items. The
trick is, your tutees can only <u>give you ten clues</u>
(e.g., "This item is under the dictionary), so
they must be prepared to be precise and to use
prepositions explicitly.

4. <u>Pick out a passage</u> from the student's textbook
or some other relevant reading material and <u>re-
write it, leaving blanks where the prepositions
are</u>. Then ask the student to fill in the blanks
and compare it with the original.

<u>Vocabulary</u>   General vocabulary errors are com-
mon for ESL students. They must acquire an English-
language vocabulary, and doing so takes time. In
college, they must also acquire a specialized vocabulary, depending on their field. Learning vocabulary
can be a frustrating experience for them. Often words
on their essays are circled and "wrong word" or "word
usage" is written in the margin. They might look a
word up and find that, according to the dictionary,
the word does not <u>seem</u> incorrect. If they complain to
the teacher, the teacher will explain, "Well, the word
is not correct in the <u>sense</u> you used it." For example, a student may write "I seek an A in this

course," because the dictionary defined "seek" as "to look for," not realizing the formality of the word. On the other hand, the dictionary might clearly show that the word was incorrectly used. "But how was I to know it wasn't the correct word?" the student wonders.

Learning a new vocabulary is a slow, painstaking process, for it is not enough to be adequate; as a student one must learn to use the language clearly, explicitly, and, depending on the course, even aesthetically. Since reading English is probably the best way to acquire an English vocabulary, many of the techniques discussed in the reading section apply also to writing. Especially useful is practicing how to figure out meaning from context and root formation. But reading is a more passive activity than writing, demanding only the ability to decode. Writing, on the other hand, necessitates encoding (which presupposes decoding). Whatever passive vocabulary has been stored by listening and reading must be activated. To do this, students must practice; they must read, speak, and listen to English as much as possible; they must write in English, and they must get feedback on what they write. Here are some effective ways of providing the necessary feedback on students' writing:

1. <u>Give your tutees as much writing experience as</u> possible. Even if they write for only ten minutes in a tutoring hour, writing in English and having their writing reviewed will help them to activate their vocabulary and give them practice in using words correctly.

2. <u>Make lists of words they will need for their</u> <u>course</u> (get this material from the textbook or syllabus) and devise questions that may be answered with short essays or even one-sentence answers that will require they use these words.

3. <u>Have them keep a list of words they have used in-</u> <u>correctly on essays or in the tutorial, and have</u> <u>them write a sentence using each of them.</u>

4. <u>Ask them to write down any words they hear or</u> <u>read that they would like to learn to use and go</u> <u>over their meaning in the tutorial.</u>

<u>Grammar: Verbs</u> As discussed previously, ESL students tend to have most of their grammar problems with verbs because verbs change so much in English and are so irregular. Whether or not you are a writing tutor, if your tutees are making a great many verb errors -- subject-verb agreement errors, or tense errors predominantly, you must determine whether they understand

50

the grammar. It is quite possible they never had an English course, or at least one that dealt with English grammar. Such a course may not be required at your college, but if it is available, and if your tutees are willing, such a course can be crucial for ESL students who want to improve their writing.

Of course, such a course would be in the future, and your students need help now. They are being marked down one, perhaps two grades because of incorrect grammar. Here are some strategies you can use to help your tutees improve their grammar:

1. If you feel confident about your knowledge of grammar, see if you can get your students a copy of a basic grammar book and look over the material about verbs, including regular conjugations in the major tenses (i.e., present, present and past perfect, past definite, future). Assign homework from the grammar book.

2. Drill your tutees on using these verbs correctly; use exercises from any grammar book or make up your own.

3. Drill your tutees on lists of irregular verb forms they have memorized.

4. See if your tutees can correct (and explain) their mistakes in graded essays or in writing

they have done for you by themselves. One way to help students correct on their own is to show them a sentence or phrase and tell them to find a similar error in their own essays. For example, you might say, "You have an error that looks like this: 'Modern medicine depend a great deal on technology.'" In asking tutees to look for this error in their own papers, you both make sure they understand the concept and that they reread their papers carefully.

5. Use controlled compositions (see p. 61) to practice subject-verb agreement and correct tense.

6. Practice proofreading techniques with your tutees so that they can learn to spot verb errors. Tell your tutees they should:

   a. underline all verbs and go back to check for tense and agreement

   b. put a piece of paper under the first line of the essay and then read it slowly, moving the paper down line by line

   c. put the paper under the last line and move the paper towards the beginning of the essay, line by line

   d. read the paper out loud to a friend, to the tutor, or to themselves

   e. listen to the tutor read a copy of the paper

slowly, while they look at another copy, and correct any errors verbally. (The tutor will not mention that he or she is correcting.)

This technique is based on the premise that if students recognize the error, they will be halfway to correcting it anyway. Note that in none of these methods do you correct (or edit) for students. As discussed in The Tutor Book, students learn by doing. If you do for them, you will not only impede their active learning but, probably, reinforce their deep fears that they could not have done it themselves.

If you are not confident about your ability to explain grammatical points, see if you can find or refer your student to a programmed grammar book. (See Bibliography.) You can still, and should, go over proofreading techniques with your tutee.

Fluency   Fluency is a word used frequently when referring to ESL proficiency . As a rule, it refers to the learner's ability to communicate, that is to decode and encode, quickly and smoothly, generally correctly. When people are fluent readers, they will rarely need to stop to look up words or figure out grammatical structures; when they are fluent speakers, people may notice their accents but will easily understand what they are saying; when they are fluent listeners, they will understand, without translating

line for line, what is being said; and if they are
fluent writers, the writing will flow smoothly and
clearly, and the reader will be generally unaware that
English is not their first language.

Both usage problems and grammar problems can
impede fluency. But the most difficult area of fluency for ESL students to attain is syntactic fluency,
that is, ease with the normal structure of the English
sentence. For example, an ESL student might write the
following sentence: "It is not in Canada, this holiday, which is a day very important for the people
American." The student has transliterated from her
own language, and the words are in the wrong order,
making the sentence sound clumsy and awkward. If too
many sentences are like this one, the essay may even
be incoherent. The smooth flow of ideas is another
aspect of fluency. If students develop fluency in
generating ideas they will become more fluent syntac-
tically.

Clearly, fluency is something gained by practice;
fluency in writing will occur for the above student if
she writes enough and her writing is corrected. However, there are some techniques you can employ to
guide your ESL students to fluency:

Free writing is an activity designed to liberate
the writer so that ideas flow freely. In its ability

to "loosen up" students' writing it can be a useful way of practicing fluency. First, pick a topic, preferably one of interest to your tutees. Second, tell them they must write for five or ten minutes without stopping and without correcting. If tutees run out of things to say, they can write, "I don't know what to say!" or "This is awful," or "Ugh, ugh, ugh." The point is, the pen must continue moving (fluently) for the entire time. Finally, when the five minutes are up, call time. Then ask your students to read the passage out loud. They will probably be surprised at the degree of fluency this writing has generated because it was, eventually, unselfconscious. Try to do this every session if your tutees have fluency problems.

Invention techniques are methods designed specifically to help people discover what they have to say about a given subject. In helping the ideas on a given topic emerge, these techniques can help your tutees to become more fluent. One particularly useful invention technique is brainstorming. In brainstorming students pick a subject (perhaps the topic of an upcoming paper) and free associate, that is, think of all the ideas that come to mind related to this topic. Tutees say these ideas out loud and you write them down, whether or not you feel they pertain to the subject or make sense. Once students have run out of ideas, ask them to try to group the ideas under categories which contain a number of similar ideas. (Some ideas may not fit under any grouping, and they can be eliminated at this time.) Finally, students may want to pick one of these categories as the basis for the thesis of the paper, or to find one thesis that connects all the categories.

Outlining can improve ESL students' fluency by giving them a measure of control over their writing, thereby guaranteeing them a degree of coherence. Students should be taught to recognize the thesis and to make certain the thesis is supported by everything else in the essay. Students should introduce the thesis, and conclude the essay. Everything in the essay should cohere. Make up an outline form, like the one on the following page, and ask your tutees to try to use it when they plan the essay. If your tutees write in drafts (and by all means, you should encourage them to write several drafts of a paper) the same form can be used as a checklist to make certain these elements are present.

Outline Form

I. Write your thesis or main idea here (there may
    be one or more sentences):_____

    _____

    _____

    _____

II. What are your strategies for introducing your
    thesis?_____

    _____

    _____

    _____

III. How will you support your thesis?
    Support 1_____

    _____

    Support 2_____

    _____

    Support 3_____

    Etc._____

IV. What are your strategies for concluding your
    essay?_____

    _____

    _____

    _____

Tell your tutees not to be discouraged if they cannot fill in the form completely. It takes years to learn how to outline and many people never learn to write that way. However, an outline can always be used after the first draft as a way of describing what one has done and learning to see and understand the essay's structure.

Sentence Combining   Often ESL students are so afraid of possible mistakes in syntax they write short, simple sentences that sound like baby talk; others try to write longer, more complicated sentences but are unsure of how to do it, and their writing sounds awkward and clumsy. Sentence combining is a method that aims to give students control over their sentences by giving them ways to use subordination, coordination, and modification to expand sentences.

To practice sentence combining with your tutees you should try to get one of the texts on the market. (See Bibliography.) If none is available, you can make up sentences like the ones below, or find sentences in students' writing that need expansion:

The girl sat in front of the fire.
The girl read her book.
The girl was young.
The girl sat on a red chair.
The fire burned steadily.

The fire was warm.

These sentences can be combined to read: The young girl sat in front of the warm fire on a red chair; while she read her book the fire burned steadily. However, there are several other combinations that are also correct, and you should encourage your tutees to try as many as possible.

In Syntactic Modelling tutees copy the syntax of a passage written by an accomplished author and, in that way, practice writing fluently and elegantly. Following is a brief example of syntactic modelling. I would advise, however, that to be of any lasting value the passage be longer and the procedure done on a regular basis.

> The man at once slung his gun over his shoulder, and came forward with the same curious swift, yet soft movement, as if keeping invisible.

> -from D.H. Lawrence, Lady Chatterly's Lover
> (New York: Bantam Books, 1968), p. 47.

Modelled, it becomes:

> The dog at once rubbed his nose on his paws, and scampered away with darting yet happy looks, as if harboring a secret.

A Controlled Composition is an essay that has already been prepared. Students are asked to change the essay in one way (a controlled way). For example, you can ask students to change the essay's tense (from present to future, or to past) to practice tense. To practice subject-verb agreement, you can ask them to change the essay from a first person point of view to a third-person point of view. You can ask students to shift their writing from the passive to the active voice or vice versa to give them practice in different syntactic structures.

SPECIAL CONCERNS

This booklet has emphasized methodologies, ways you, the tutor, can help your ESL students compensate for difficulties with the English language, while still concentrating on the specific subject you tutor. What has not been explored are two extra-linguistic factors which could contribute to ESL students' linguistic difficulties. They are briefly outlined below:

Lack of Competence in Native Language

Much of what has been suggested in this booklet is based on the premise that your tutees have attained a certain degree of literacy in their first language: that is, they can read and write competently in their native language. In actuality, such first-language competence does not always exist. Many ESL students, although in college, have never attained a high level of linguistic ability. Many can speak their language quite fluently and expressively, since speaking was essential for survival. However, they may have received little formal schooling and, hence, never learned to read and write particularly well. Some

ESL students came to this country when they were still in grammar school; so their education was incomplete in their native language.

These students will have additional problems with English. Although speaking it may come easily to them, at least if they have been in this country awhile, writing and reading it will be extra difficult because they have never, or only imperfectly, learned to read and write. Had they learned it earlier, when they were five or six, it would have been easier. Now, older, after perhaps some frustrating and negative experiences, English may be a humiliating and difficult ordeal for them.

These students should be receiving some compensatory aid. They should be in basic skills courses (i.e., remedial or developmental reading and writing) and they should be getting tutoring in reading and writing. If there are no such programs at your school, you should speak to your supervisor and ask him or her to find out if any financial programs are available to fund private tutoring. You cannot, alone, compensate and cannot be expected to. You are not an ESL specialist, and perhaps are not expert in reading or writing either. Your job is to help the student learn the subject you tutor. Try not to feel frustrated or helpless yourself.

Psychological Considerations

The mind does not operate in a vacuum. When we learn languages, there are other factors helping or impeding our learning besides native intellectual faculties. Your ESL tutees may well feel more uncertain and insecure about their ability to perform well in college than your native-speaking tutees. Some were fluent, perhaps learned, in their own culture and suddenly have been put in a position where they have difficulty understanding and communicating what they do or do not understand. In some schools they are placed in remedial, basic skills classes and are labelled, or feel themselves labelled intellectually inferior. They may fail some courses because of their language deficiency.

Those who have not received formal education in their own language or in English have come to college hoping to make up for their academic deficiencies. However, what they too often meet is failure and frustration. It takes longer to learn an academic subject when one is just beginning to master the linguistic tools needed to communicate one's knowledge. And most colleges do not have all the support systems -- developmental courses, tutorial and counseling services -- required to help those students compensate for poor language skills. Thus, you may find your tutees more insecure or angry than seems warranted by their actual performance or their ability to perform.

Another psychological reaction to being a second language learner is insulation. Foreign-born ESL students have come to this country for a multitude of reasons. Some are here only for an education, and these students probably welcome the chance to learn about a new culture along with a new language. However, many are here for political or economic reasons and cannot easily return to their native countries. These students are also anxious to function well in their new culture and new language; however, survival in this society may well represent to them annihilation of their native culture. Unconsciously, they may resist learning English from the fear that becoming fluent in English will mean assimilating culturally, and, thus, losing all contact with their native culture.

Some colleges have worked with this problem by developing bilingual education programs so that students can study in both their native language and in English. Other colleges have instituted culture clubs to celebrate cultural origins. However, these measures are, by their very nature, transitional. Eventually ESL students must recognize the reality of their situation, including the fact that the only way to learn English well is to immerse oneself in the language and culture: listening in English, conversing in English, reading in English, and writing in English.

As their tutor what can you do to help your ESL students handle the psychological trauma that may accompany their learning English? Understanding goes a long way -- listening to them and allowing (even encouraging) them to voice their hopes and fears is crucial. Mainly, you can reinforce what they are actually accomplishing academically; help them to see that, although it is taking longer than they had thought it would, they are making progress. Also, help them to see that they do not need to <u>lose</u> their native culture, that one does not lose a language one has spoken for eighteen-odd years, nor the culture in which one is raised. Most of all, be patient and sensitive to cultural differences and don't be discouraged by all that needs to be done. Set reasonable goals with your tutee; you cannot do everything in one term.

ANNOTATED BIBLIOGRAPHY

Arkin, Marian, Paul Arenson, and Linda Rios. "Tutor-
    ing Writing to Second Language Learners: A
    Handbook" (unpublished, 1978).

Bright, J.A. and G.P.M. McGregor. Teaching English as
    a Second Language. London: Longman Group,
    1970. Practice and techniques of teaching inter-
    mediate and advanced ESL.

Brooks, G., and J. Withrow. 10 Steps: Controlled
    Composition for Beginning and Intermediate ESL
    Students. New York: Language Innovations, 1974.

Brown, J.I. Programmed Vocabulary, 2nd ed. Englewood
    Cliffs, New Jersey: Prentice-Hall, 1971.

Byrne, Donn, ed. English Teaching Perspectives. Lon-
    don: Longman Group, 1980. Collection of
    current articles on teaching ESL/EFL.

Celce-Murcia, Marianne and Lois McIntosh, eds. Teach-
    ing English as a Second or Foreign Language.
    Rowley, Massachusetts: Newbury House, 1979.
    Current articles on ESL/EFL teaching.

Dakin, Julian. The Language Laboratory and Language
    Learning. London: Longman Group, 1973.
    Methods of preparing drills and exercises for the
    language laboratory and examples of such mate-
    rial.

Dowling, Gretchen. "Tutors' Manual for LaGuardia
    Community College ESL Lab" (unpublished, 1980).

Epes, M., C. Kirkpatrick, and M. Southwell. COMP-Lab
    Exercises. Englewood Cliffs, New Jersey: Pren-
    tice-Hall, 1980. A programmed developmental
    grammar text; accompanying cassette tapes are
    also available.

Fassler, Doris and Nancy Duke Lay. Encounter with a
    New World. Englewood Cliffs, New Jersey: Pren-
    tice Hall, 1979. A composition text for ad-
    vanced ESL students.

Fawcett, Susan, and Alvin Sandberg. Grassroots: The
    Writer's Workbook. Boston: Houghton-Mifflin,
    1976. A developmental grammar workbook which
    comes in two, A and B, forms.

Ferreira, Linda A. Verbs in Action. Rowley, Massa-
    chusetts: Newbury House, 1978. Intermediate
    verb drills.

Gallingane, Gloria and Don Byrd. Write Away. New
    York: Collier Macmillan, 1977. Beginning
    level sentence-combining exercises.

Haycraft, John. An Introduction to English Language
    Teaching. London: Longman Group, 1978.
    Approaches and techniques for teaching ESL.

Kunz, Linda A. 26 Steps: Controlled Composition for
    Intermediate and Advanced ESL Students. New
    York: Language Innovations, 1972. (Rev. edi-
    tion, 1979.) An accompanying teacher's manual
    can guide you in using this compact text.

Papalia, Anthony. Learner-Centered Language Teaching:
    Methods and Materials. Rowley, Massachusetts:
    Newbury House, 1976.

Paulston, Christina Bratt and Mary Newton Bruder.
    Teaching English as a Second Language: Tech-
    niques and Procedures. Cambridge, Massachu-
    setts: Winthrop Publishers, 1976.

Rivers, Wilga M., and Mary S. Temperley. A Practical
    Guide to the Teaching of English as a Second or
    Foreign Language. New York: Oxford University
    Press, 1978. Background, strategies and
    approaches to ESL/EFL teaching.

Stevick, Earl. Memory, Meaning and Method. Rowley,
    Massachusetts: Newbury House, 1976. Discussion
    of psychological and linguistic aspects of lan-
    guage learning.

Strong, W. Sentence Combining: A Composing Book.
    New York: Russell Sage Foundation, 1973. Col-
    lege-level sentence combining exercises.

Trillin, Alice Stewart and Assoc. Teaching Basic
    Skills in College. San Francisco: Jossey Bass
    Publishers, 1980. An analysis of basic skills
    programs in writing, reading, ESL and mathemat-
    ics.

Troyka, Linda and J. Nudelman. Taking Action: Writing, Reading, Speaking, and Listening through Simulation Games. Englewood Cliffs, New Jersey: Prentice-Hall, 1975. A communication skills textbook for advanced ESL and developmental students.

Wattenmaker, Beverly S., and Virginia Wilson. A Guidebook for Teaching English as a Second Language. Boston: Allyn & Bacon, 1980. A teacher's guide and classroom exercises for teaching ESL.

Wohl, Milton. Preparation for Writing: Grammar. Rowley, Massachusetts: Newbury House, 1978. Practice in areas of grammar especially problematic for ESL students.

Wohl, Milton. Techniques for Writing: Composition. Rowley, Massachusetts: Newbury House, 1978. Practice in grammar and basic writing techniques for ESL students.

Yorkey, M. Study Skills for Students of English as a Second Language. New York: McGraw-Hill, 1970.